There will always be…

A Pony Named Midnight

Written and Illustrated
By
Jean M. Jeske

FOURTH PRINTING

Printed in the United States of America
Published by Drafty Manor
ISBN 978-0-6926-1655-0

To my daughter Jennifer
and her first pony

I THINK I'm going to LIKE MY NEW OWNER
I KNOW SHE LIKES ME
SMACK
HOPE SHE KNOWS HOW TO...
HELP!
HOW TO BRIDLE

I TINK SHE NEEDS MORE PRACTICE ON SHARP TURNS!

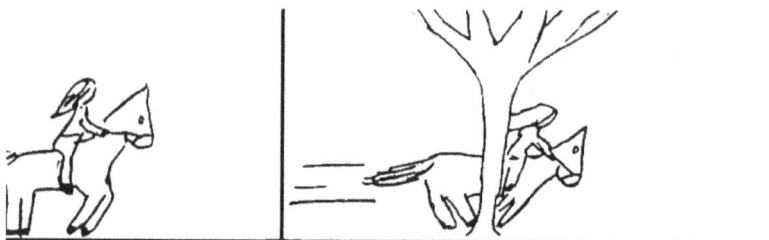

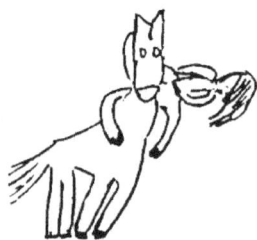

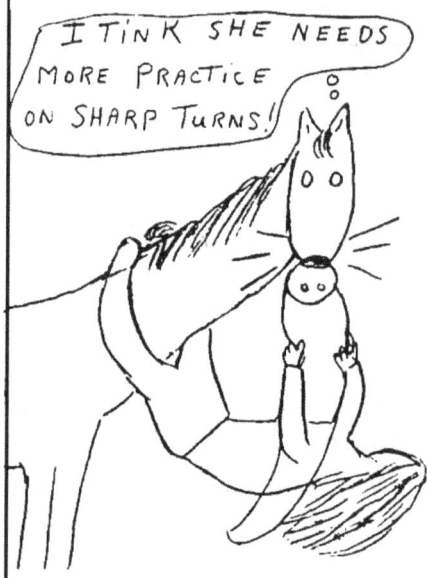

COME PLEASE
Hup?
BACK?
HOW DID I DO THIS?
DAddy!!

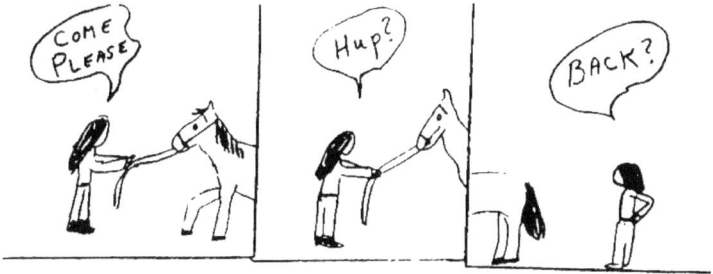

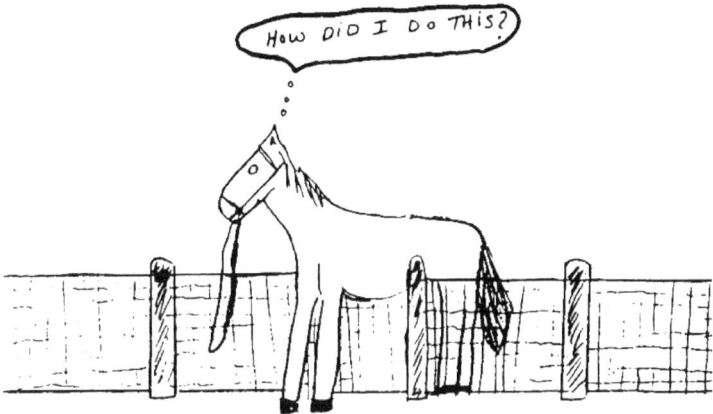

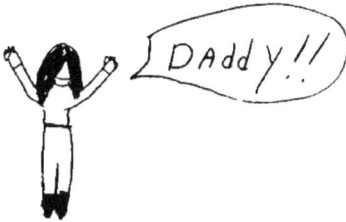

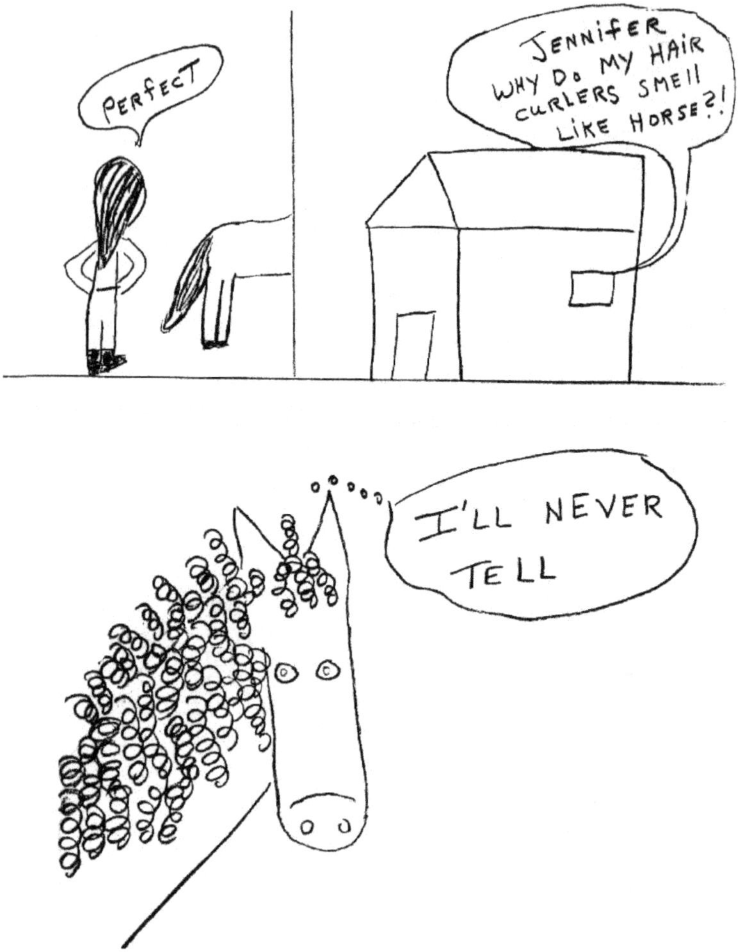
PERFECT
JENNIFER WHY DO MY HAIR CURLERS SMEll LIKE HORSE?!
I'LL NEVER TELL

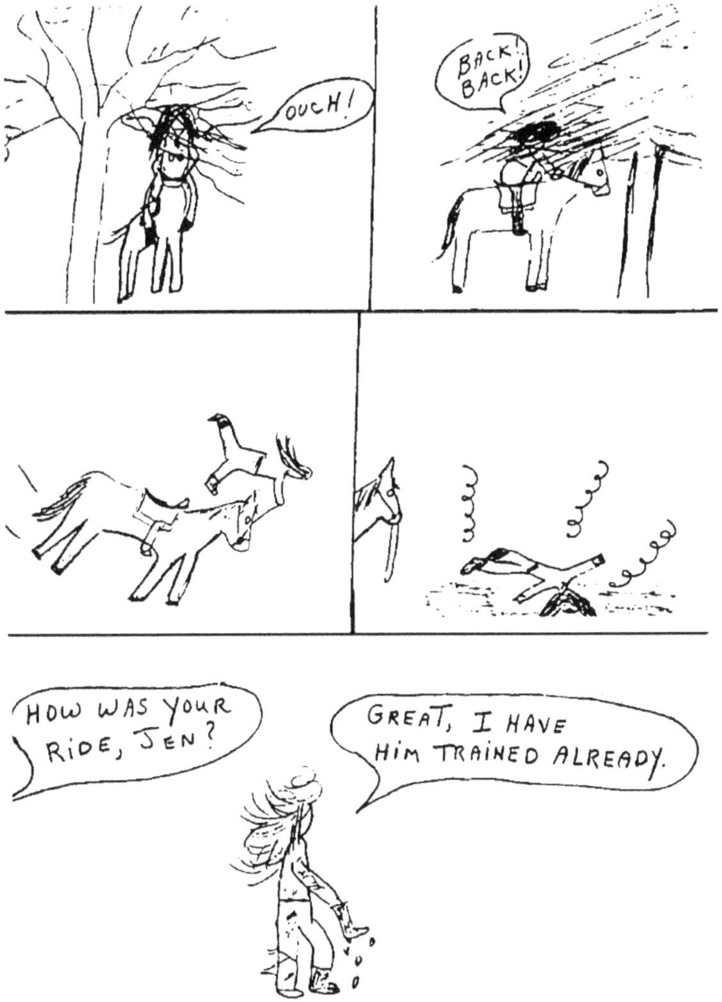
OUCH!
BACK! BACK!
HOW WAS YOUR RIDE, JEN?
GREAT, I HAVE HIM TRAINED ALREADY.

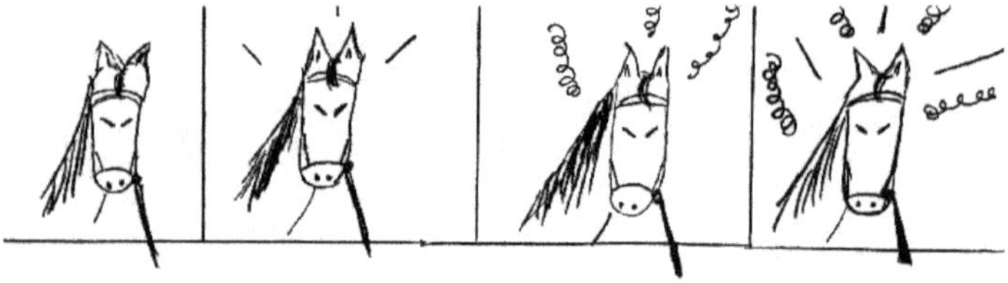

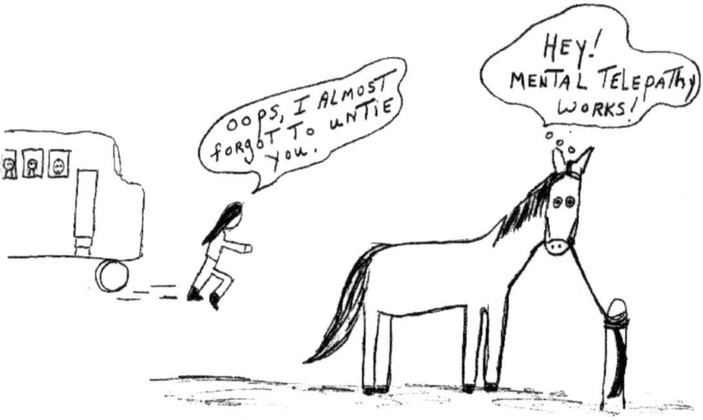
OOPS, I ALMOST forgot TO UNTIE YOU.
HEY! MENTAL TELEPATHY WORKS!

Z Z Z
Z Z Z
Z Z
Z Z Z
Z Z
Z Z
?
IT'S SO NICE TO WAKE UP ALONG SIDE OF THE ONE YOU LOVE

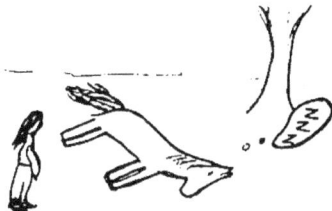

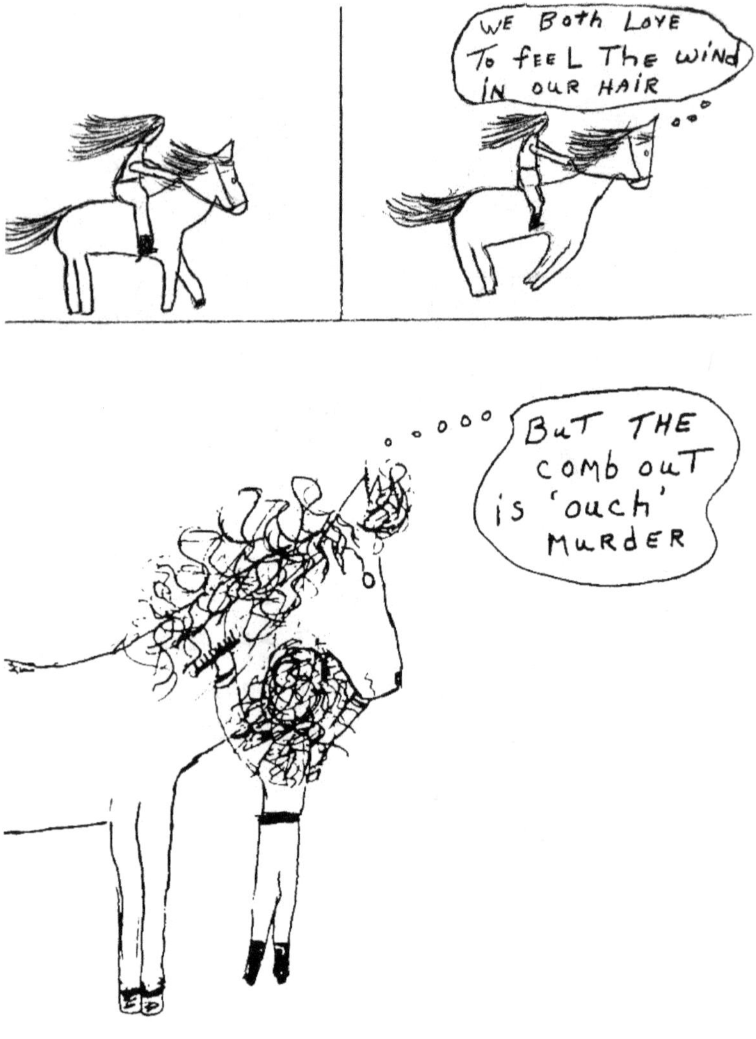
WE Both LOVE To feeL The wind iN OUR HAIR
BuT THE comb ouT is 'ouch' MuRdER

I CAN do IT MYSELF!
SHE THINKS I'M A BABY.
U
MA!

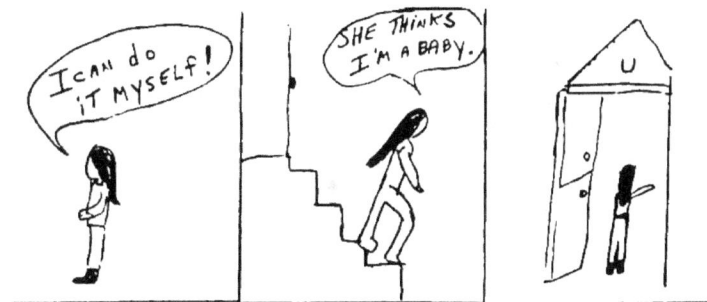

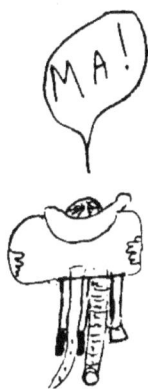

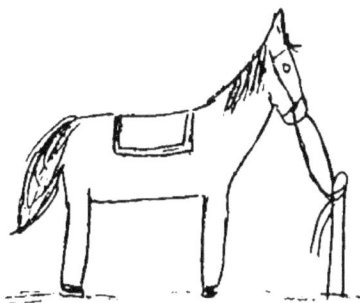

WHAT WAS THAT ALL ABOUT?!
I KNOW it's SILLY, BUT I'M AFRAID of BEES

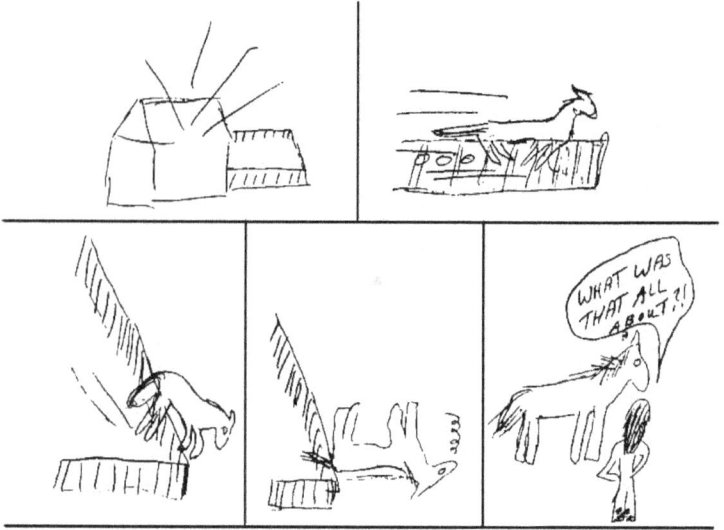

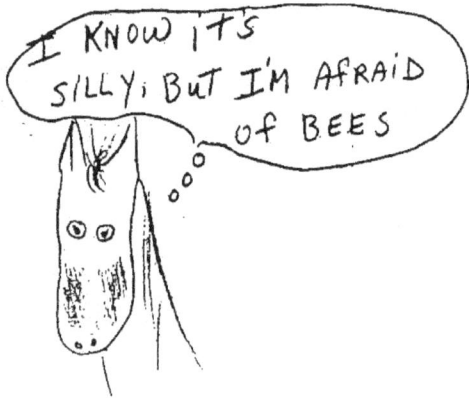

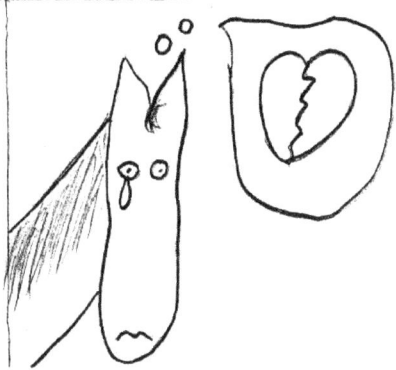

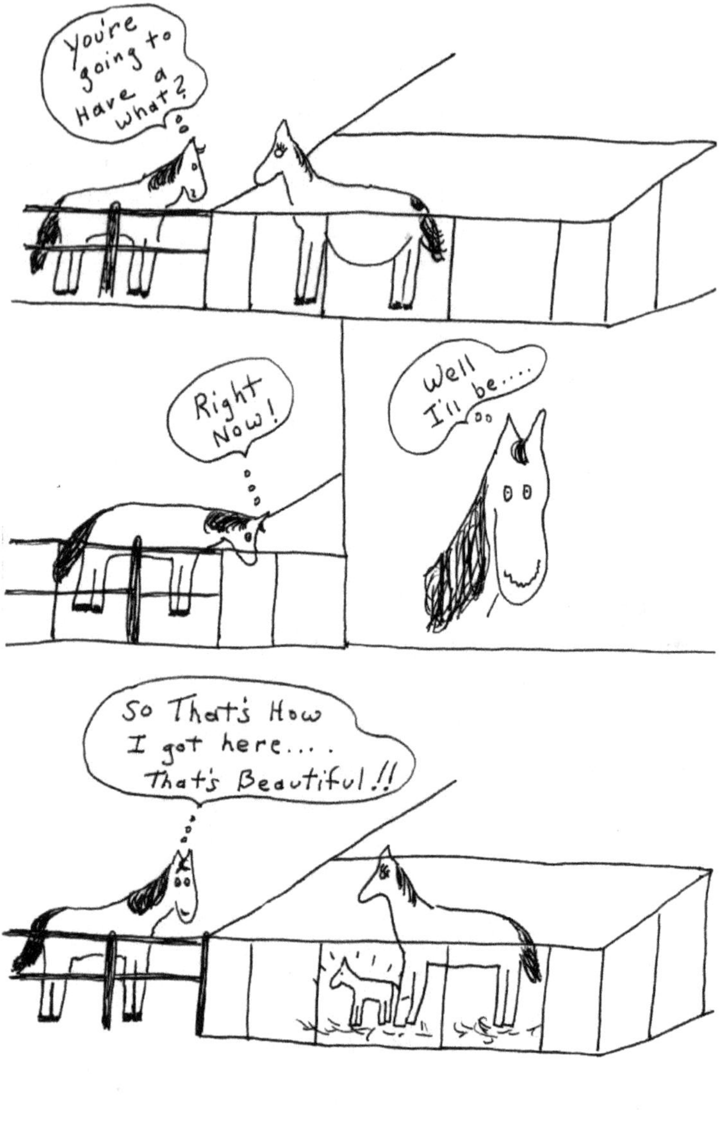
You're going to Have a what?
Right Now!
Well I'll be....
So That's How I got here.... That's Beautiful!!

?
?
?
MY RighT SIDE is definitLy MY BEST ProfiLE

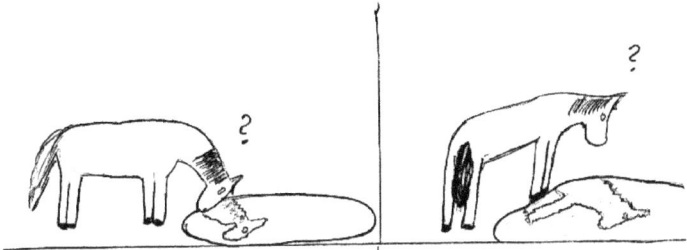

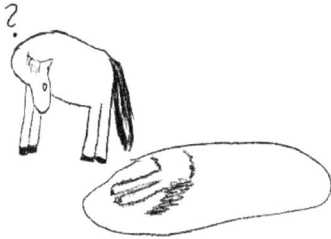

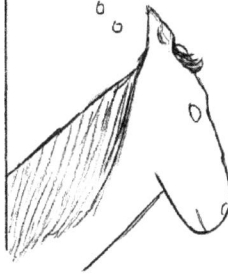

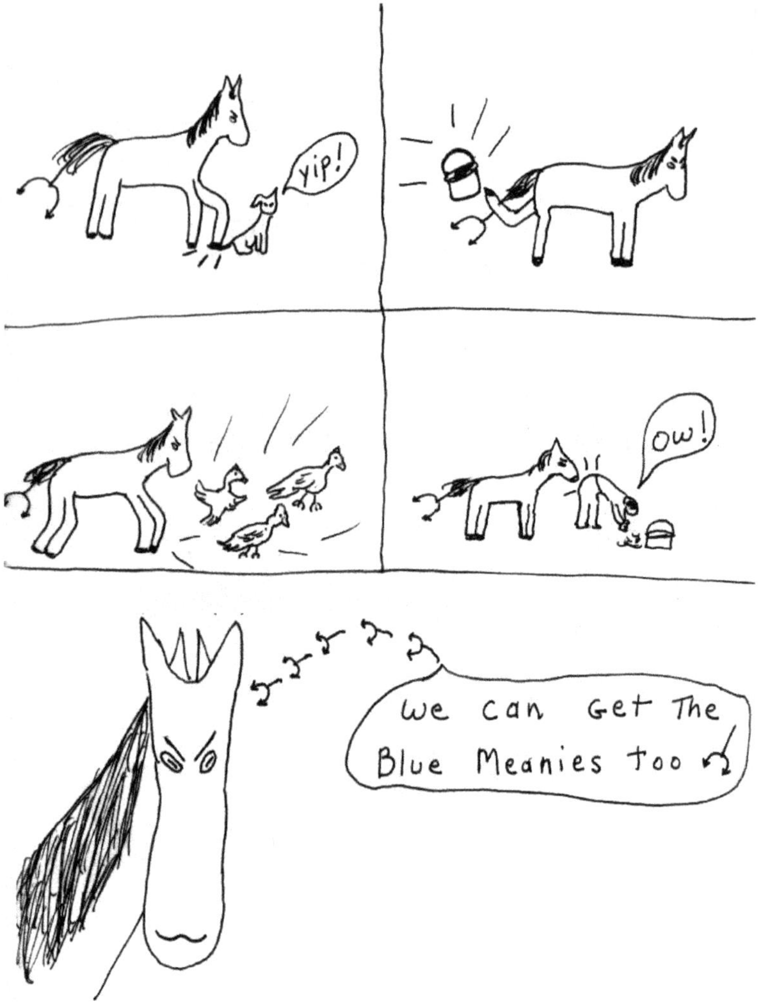
yip!
ow!
We can Get The Blue Meanies too

?
?
BLAH
ICK!
HOW CAN ANYONE CHEW Their fingerNAILs?

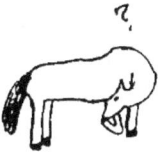

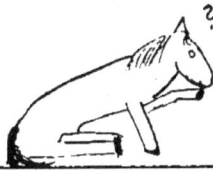

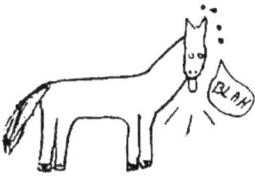

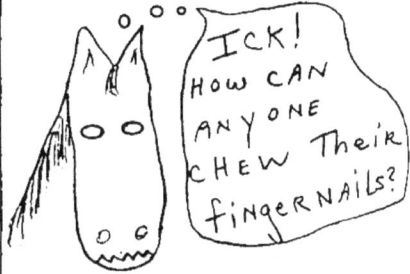

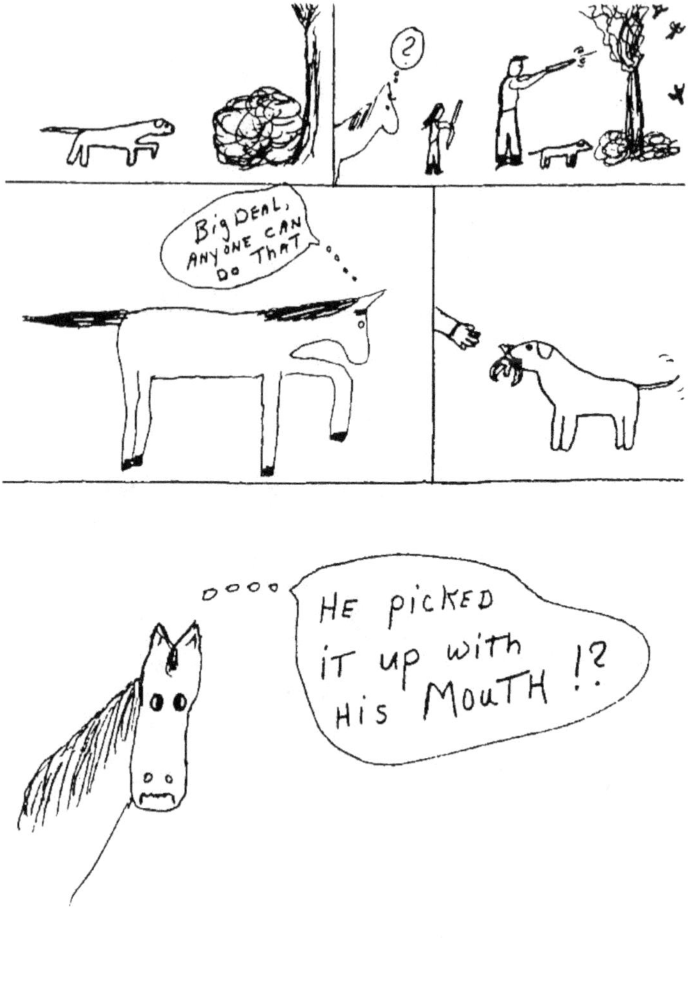
?
Big DEAL, ANYONE CAN DO THAT
HE picKED iT up with His MouTH !?

YUK! HAVE YOU EVER 'TASTED' A WIGGLY BUG?

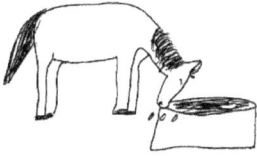

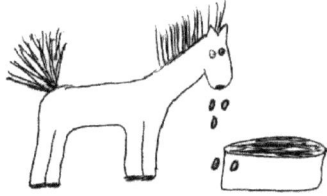

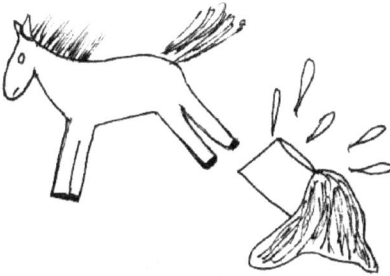

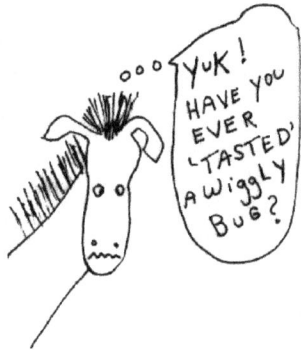

?
?
?
PERSONALLY, I don't SEE HOW THAT BEAGLE does iT

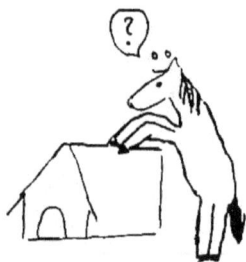

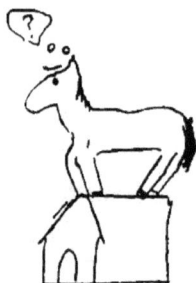

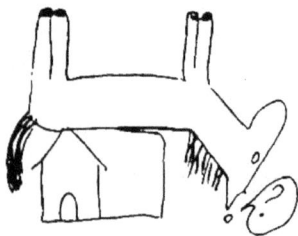

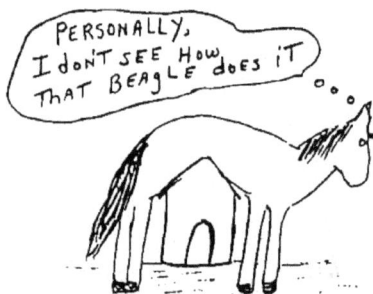

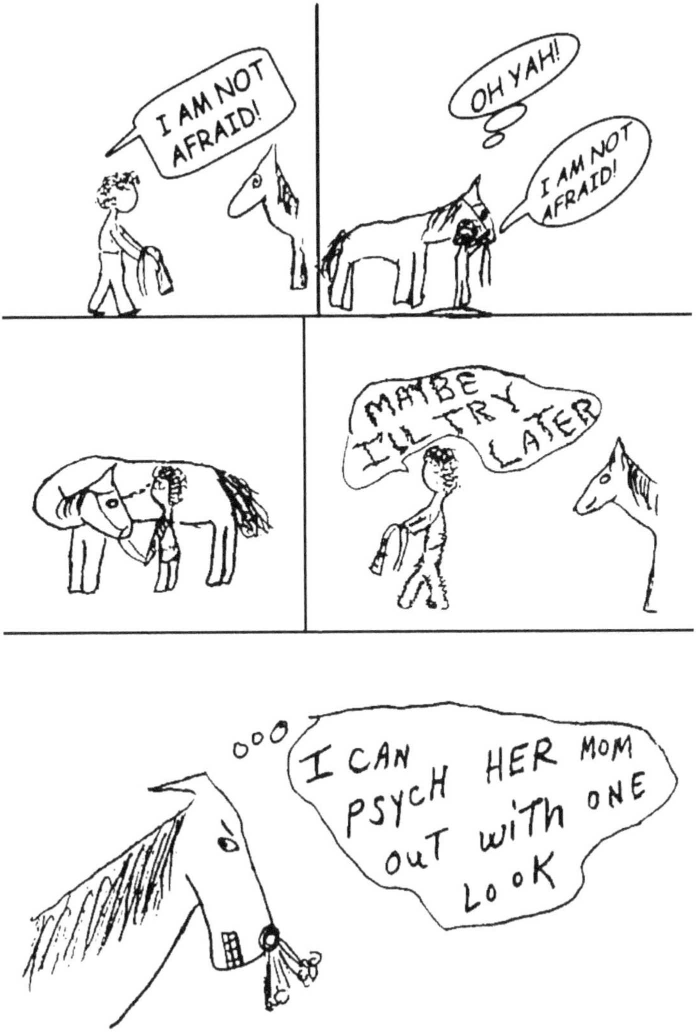
I AM NOT AFRAID!
OH YAH!
I AM NOT AFRAID!
MAYBE I'LL TRY LATER
I CAN PSYCH HER MOM OUT WITH ONE LOOK

1

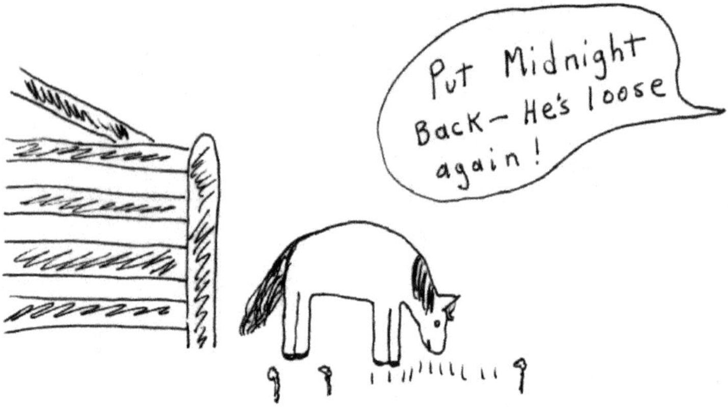
Put Midnight Back— He's loose again!

2

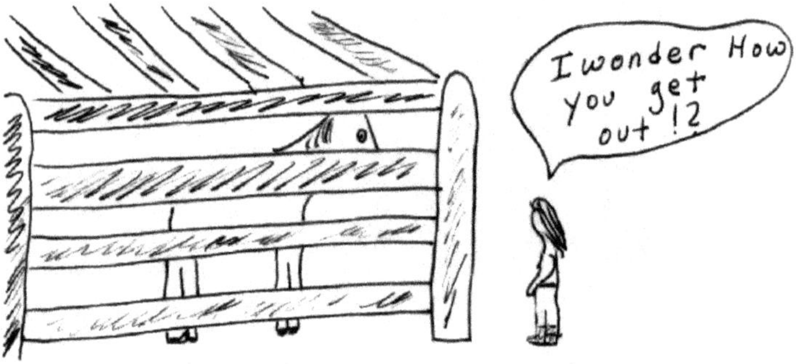
I wonder How you get out !?

3

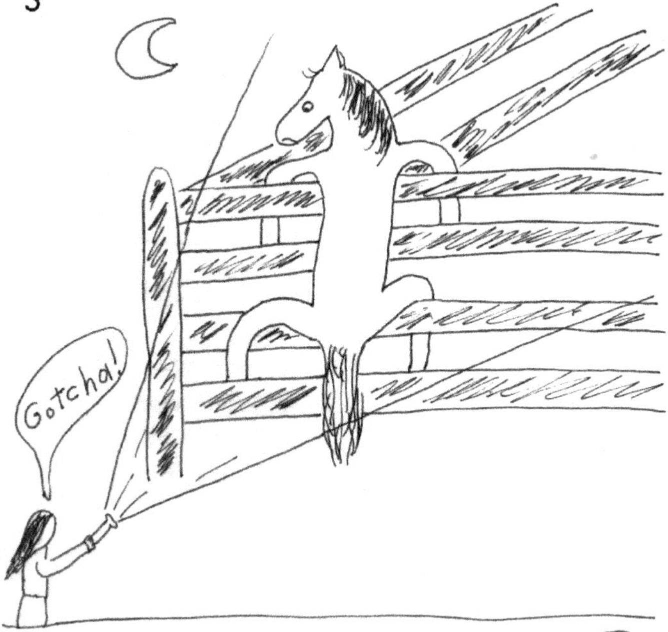
Gotcha!

4

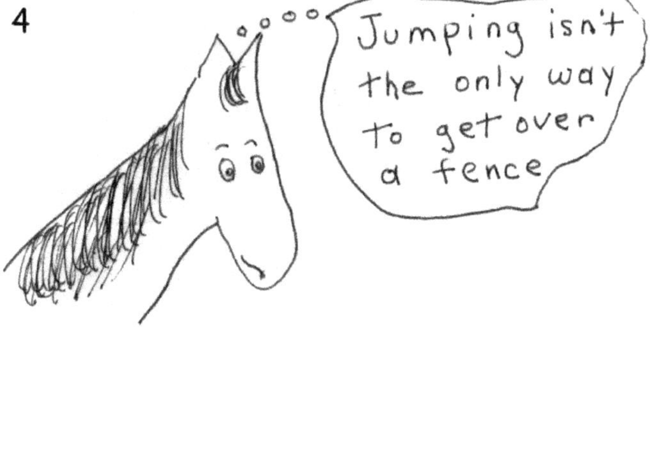
Jumping isn't the only way to get over a fence

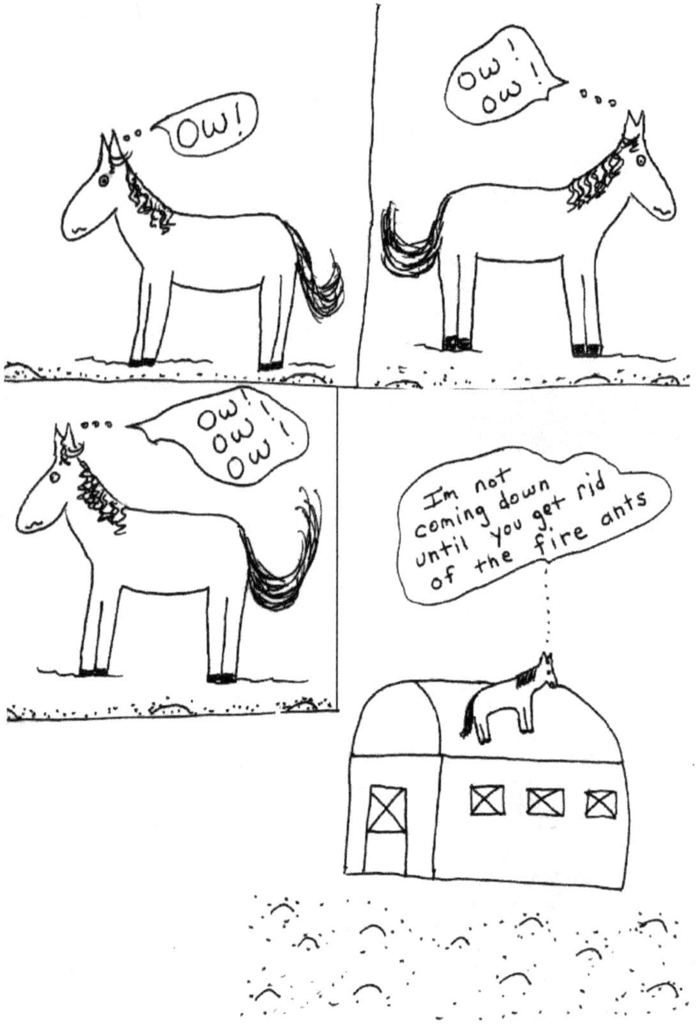
Ow!
Ow! Ow!
Ow! Ow! Ow!
I'm not coming down until you get rid of the fire ants

OUCH
OUCH
HEY. THERE
ARE STICKERS
IN THESE BUSHES!
COME ON!
FASTER!
OUCH!
HEY THERE ARE
STICKERS IN
THESE
BUSHES

REALLY??

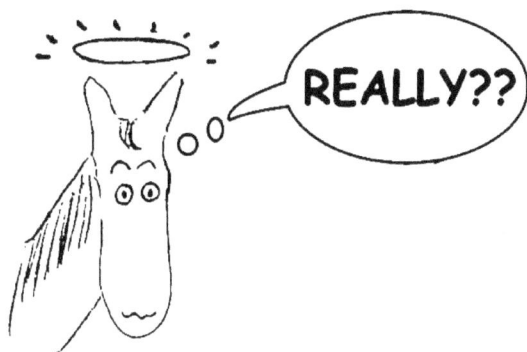

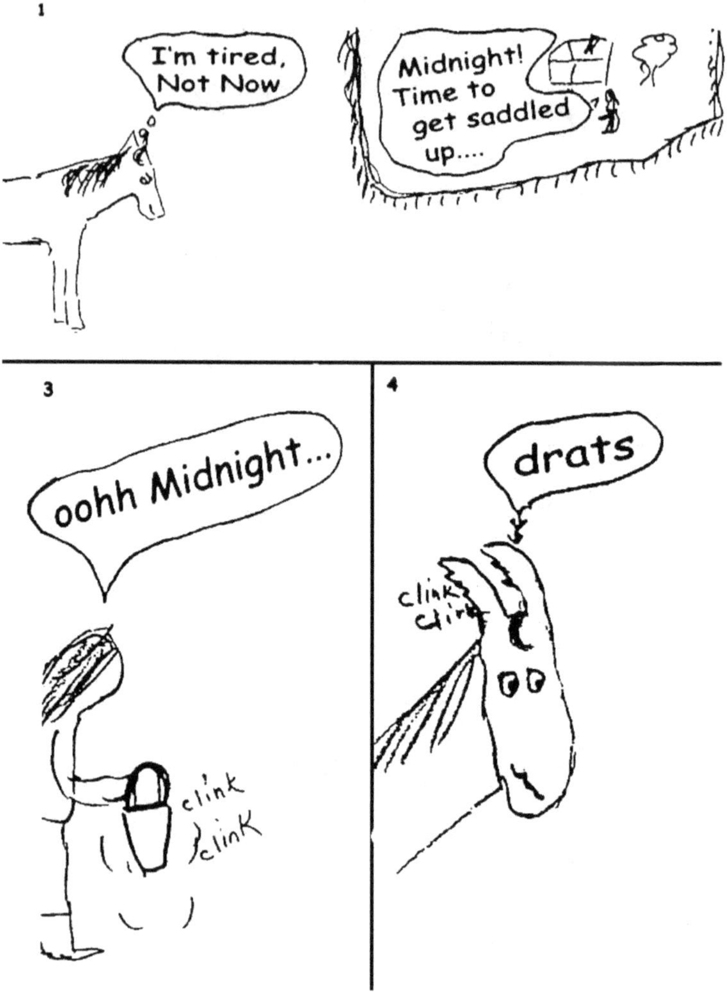
1
I'm tired, Not Now
Midnight! Time to get saddled up....
3
oohh Midnight...
clink
clink
4
drats

2

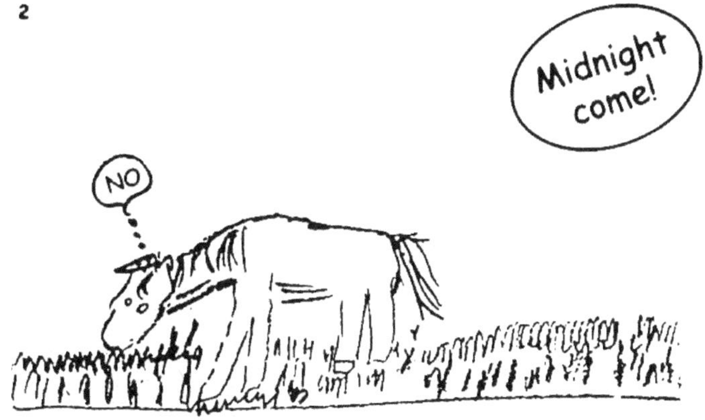
Midnight come!
NO

5

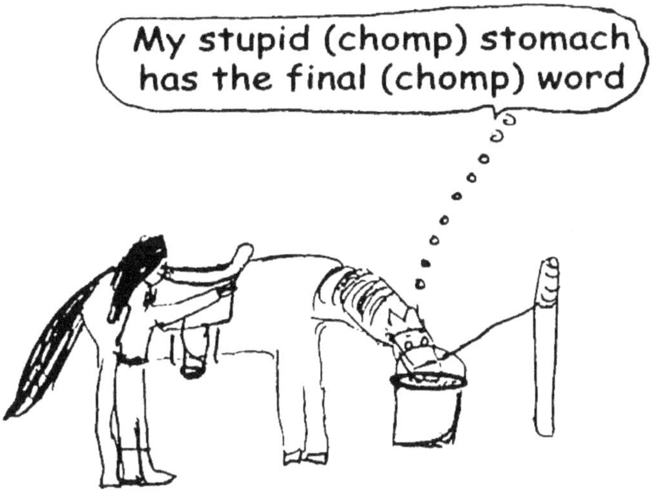
My stupid (chomp) stomach has the final (chomp) word

1
2
5
6
JENS ROOM

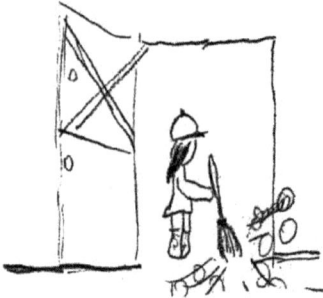

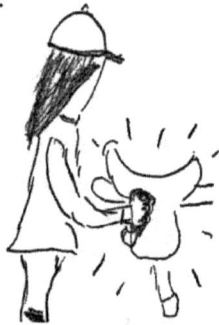

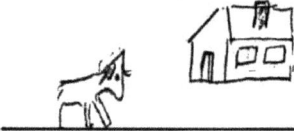

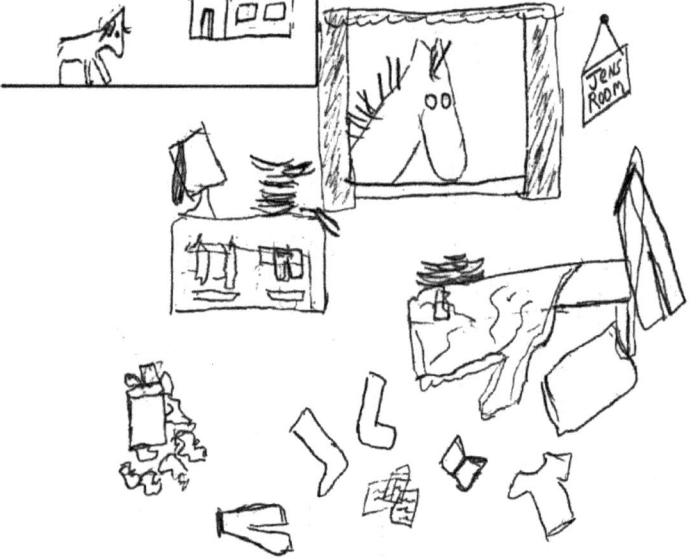

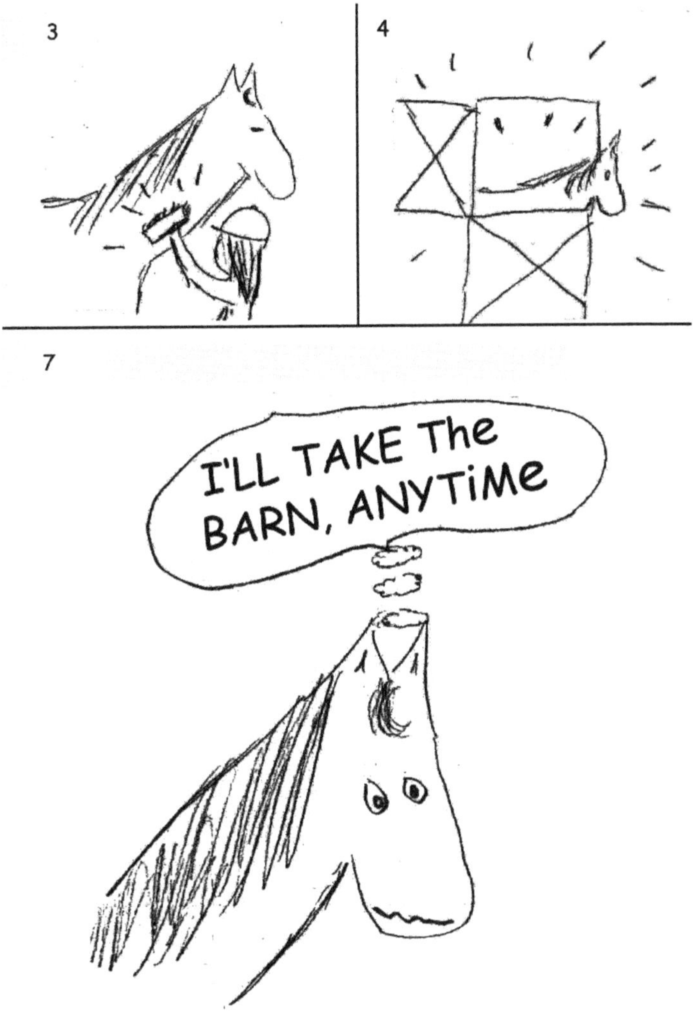
3
4
7
I'LL TAKE The BARN, ANYTiMe

?
Bzzzz
Bzzzz ooo
AH... Do you Know what you are doing?
HEY! NOT SO SHORT...
Bzzzz
yipes!

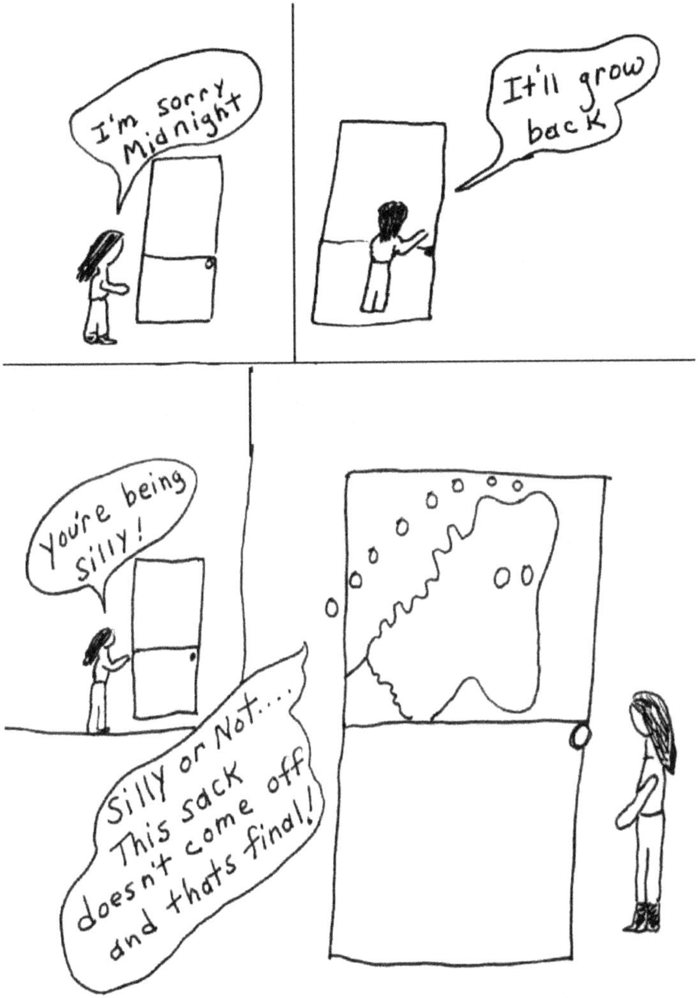
I'm sorry Midnight
It'll grow back
You're being silly!
Silly or Not.... This sack doesn't come off and thats final!!

1

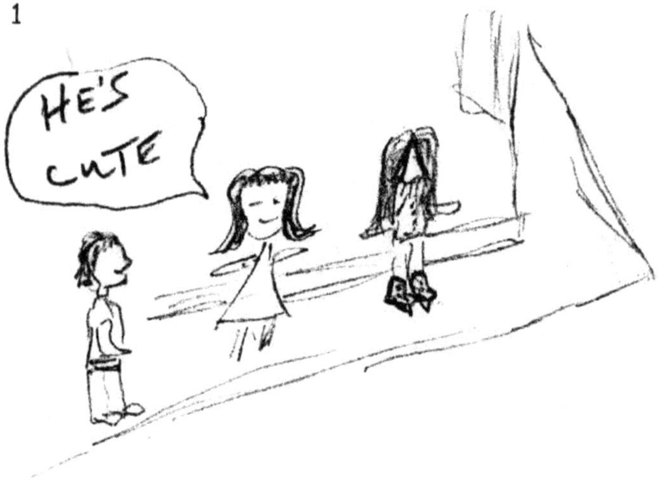
HE'S CUTE

4

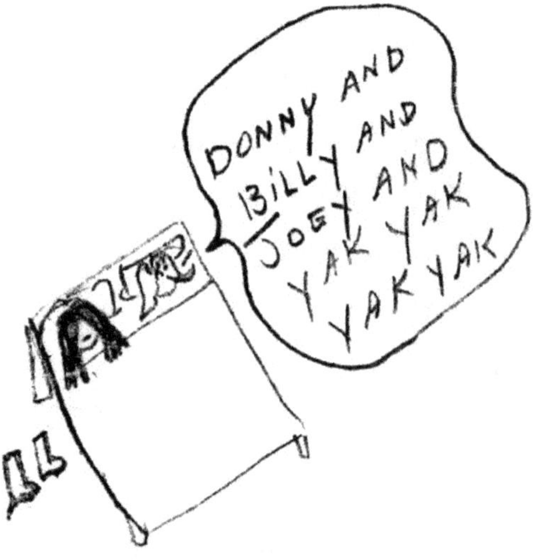
DONNY AND BILLY AND JOEY AND YAK YAK YAK YAK

2
I LiKE CURLY HAIR
3
OOH... BROAD SHOULDERS
5
MiDNigHT YOU WOULDN'T BELIEVE HOW SiLLy giRLS CAN BE.

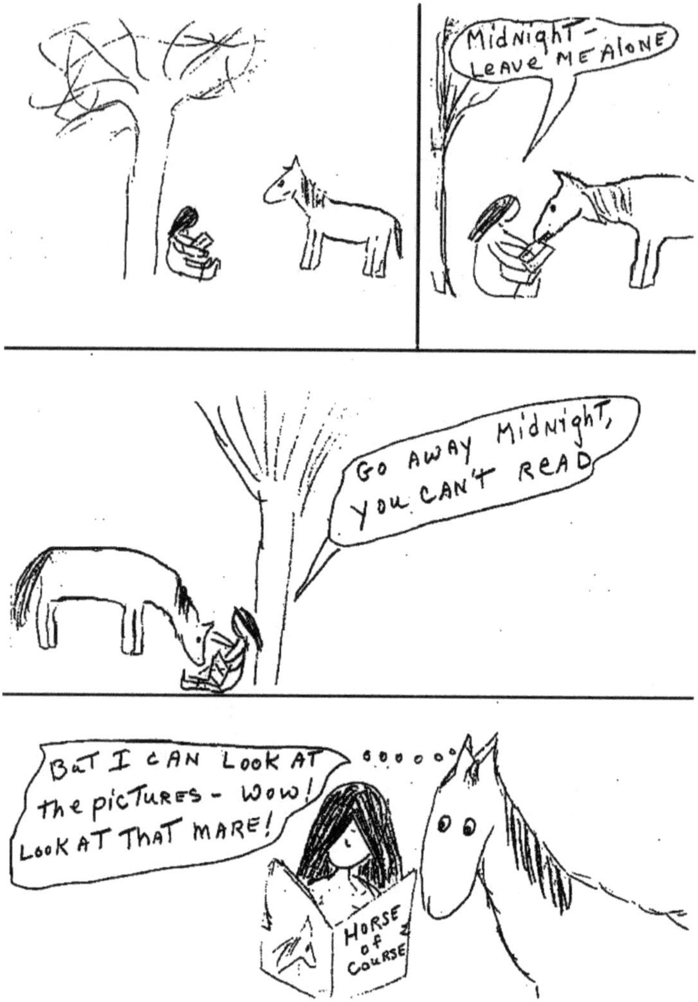
Midnight - Leave ME ALONE
GO AWAY MIDNIGHT, YOU CAN'T READ
BUT I CAN LOOK AT the picTURES - WOW! LOOK AT THAT MARE!
HORSE of COURSE

SOMEONE BETTER TEACH THAT KID HOW TO LAY DOWN!

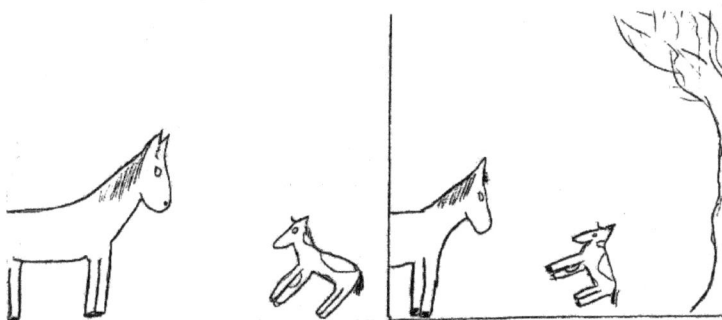

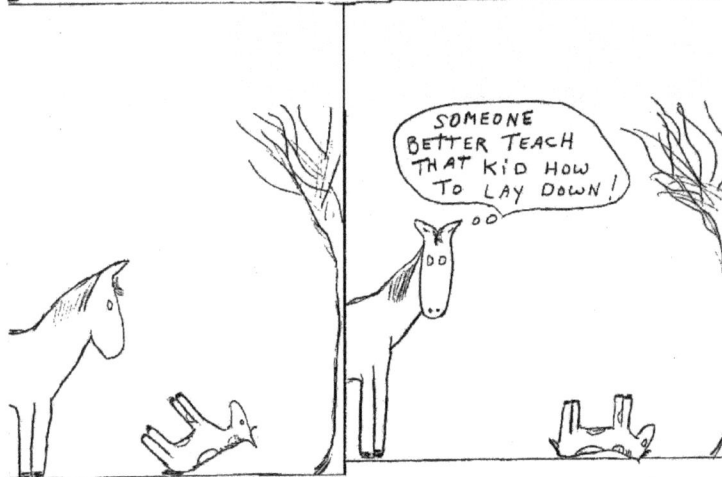

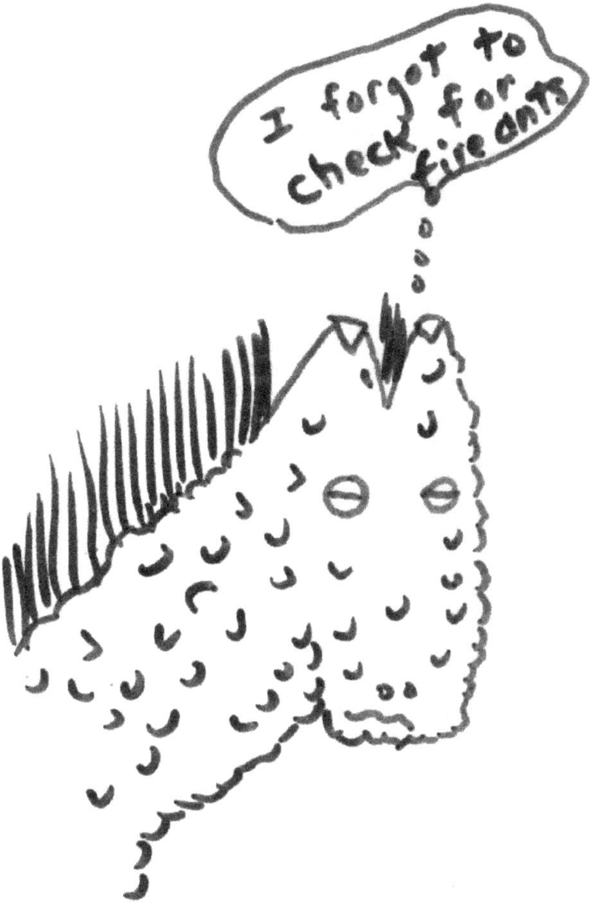
I forgot to check for fire ants

1.
?
BRING LAdy over HeRE JeNNY
2.
SURE is A cuTe MiNATURE pONY.
3.
MiNATURE MY Hoof - She's A DWARf!

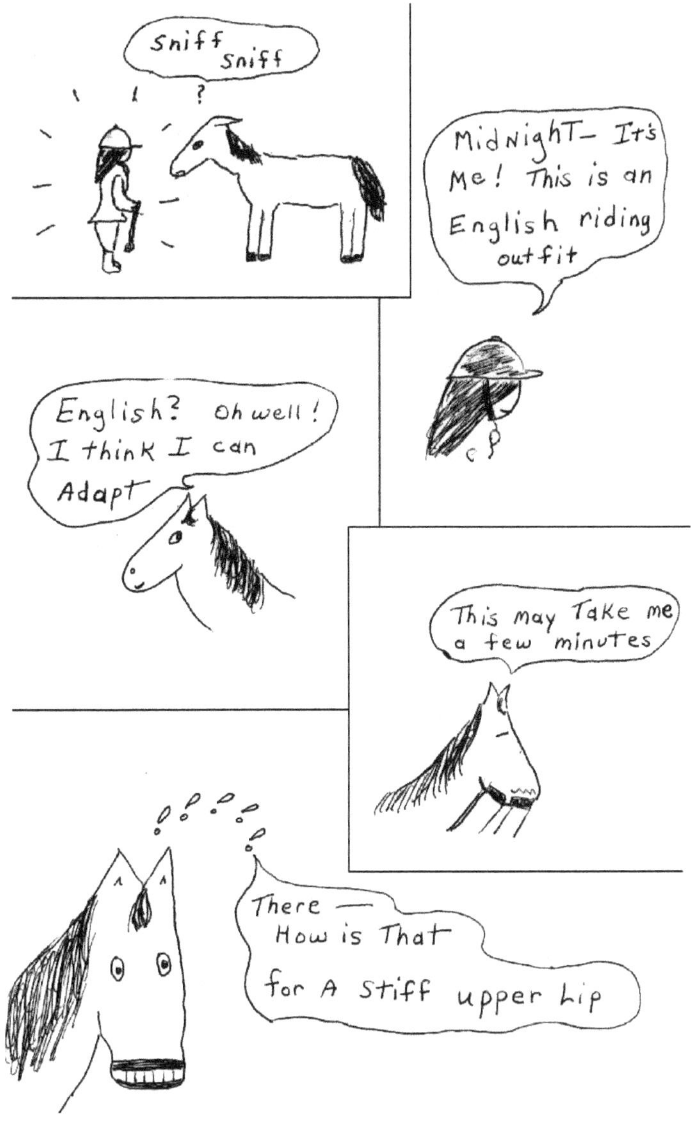
Sniff sniff
?
MidNighT– It's Me! This is an English riding outfit
English? Oh well! I think I can Adapt
This may Take me a few minutes
There — How is That for A Stiff upper Lip

Let me guess.. Your first time in a trailer?

Surprised? Well I don't like watermelon seeds either

1

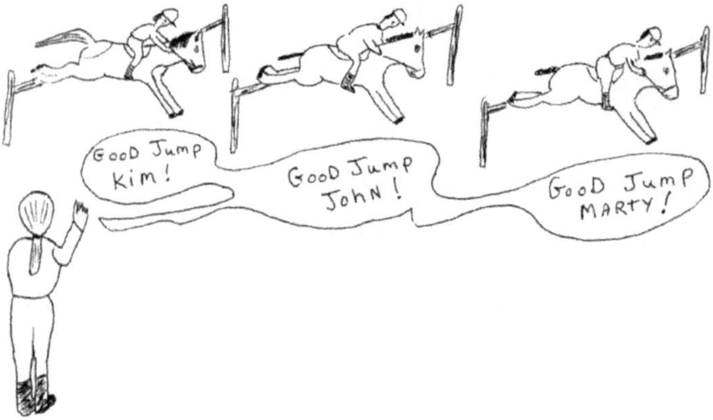
GooD Jump Kim!
GooD Jump JohN!
GooD Jump MARTY!

2

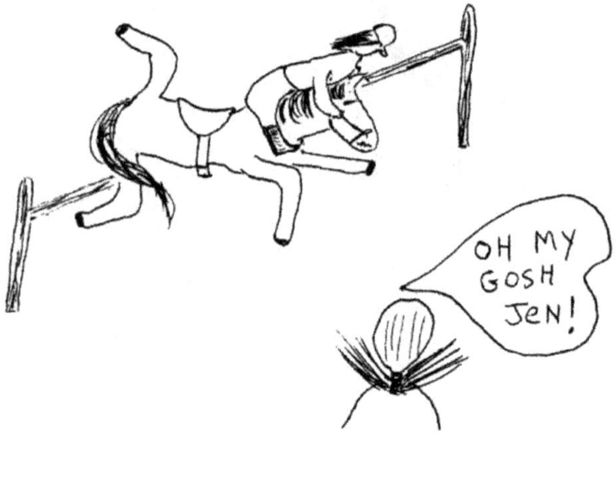
OH MY GOSH JEN!

3.

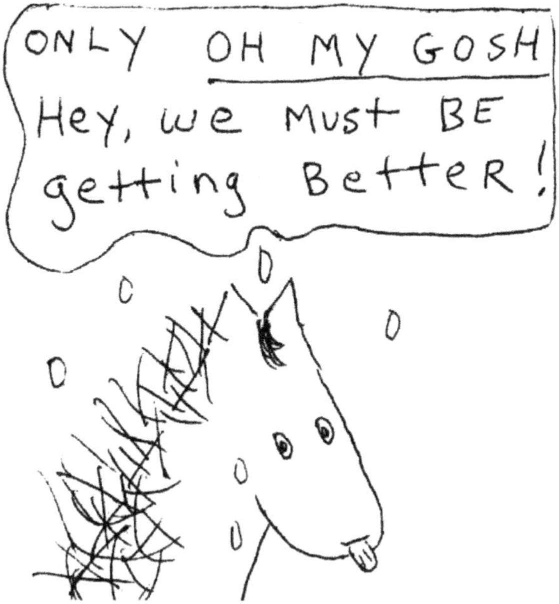
ONLY OH MY GOSH
Hey, we Must BE getting Better!

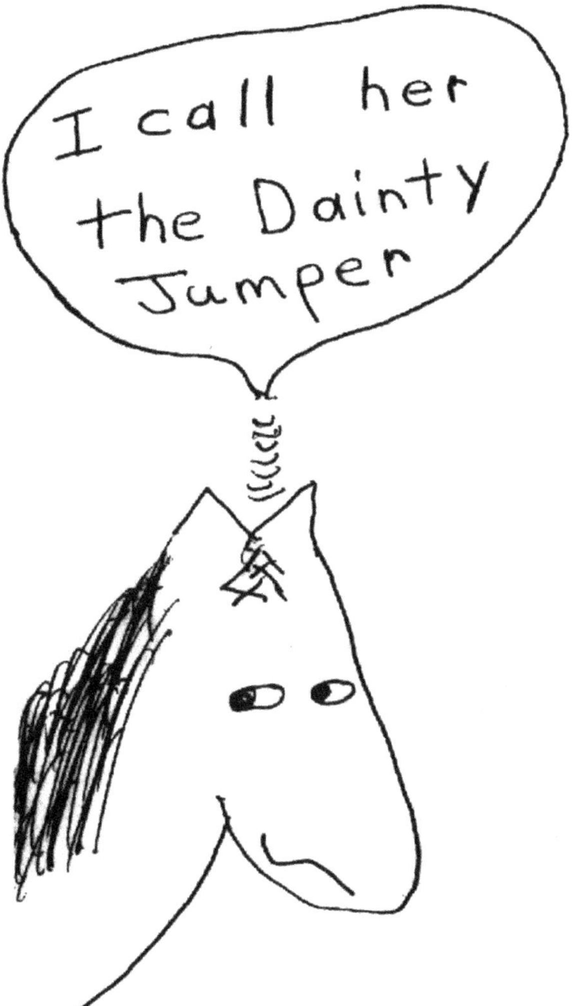
I call her the Dainty Jumper

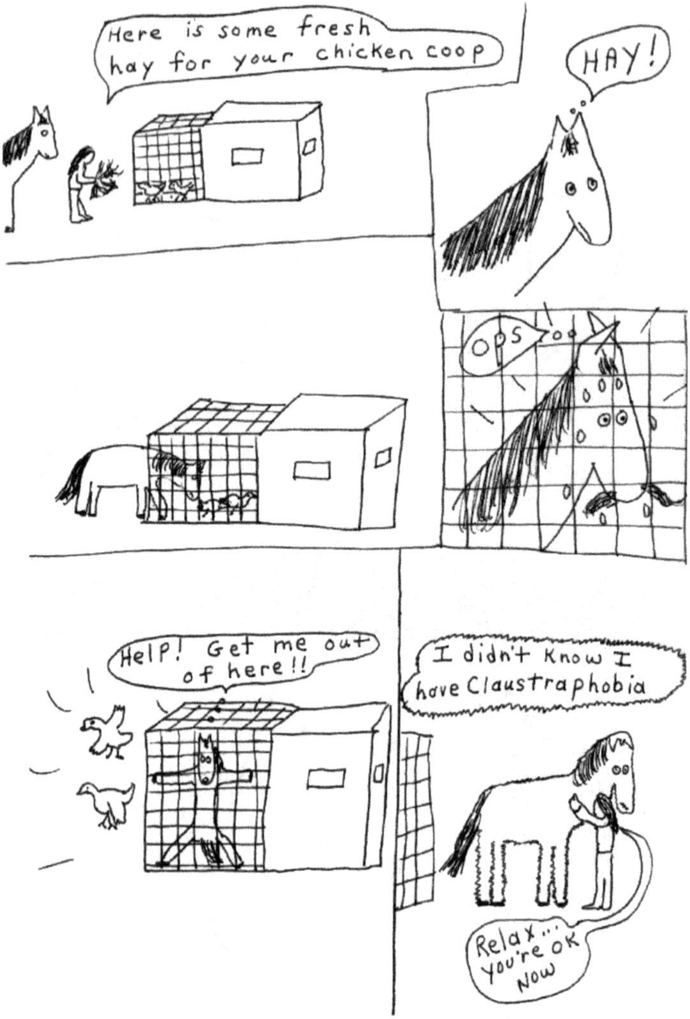
Here is some fresh hay for your chicken coop
HAY!
OPS
Help! Get me out of here!!
I didn't know I have Claustraphobia
Relax... you're OK now

OH YAH!
Beat it Kid
OH YAH!!
Scram
These Kid stallions are a pain.....
OH YAH! Let me go!

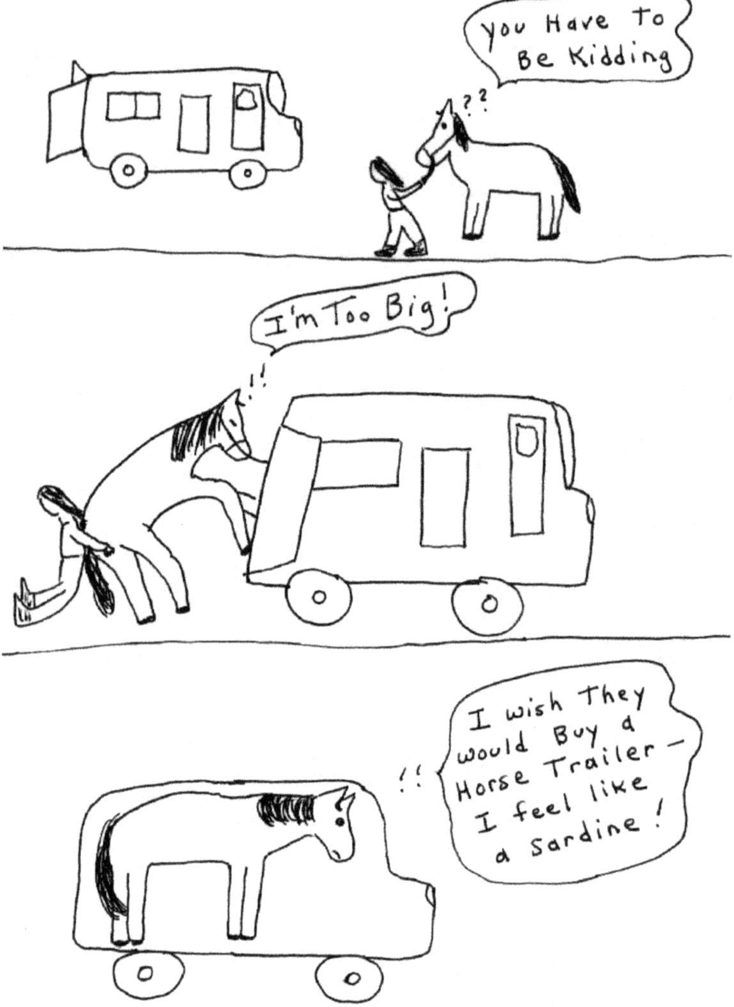
you Have to Be Kidding
??
I'm Too Big!
!!
I wish They would Buy a Horse Trailer — I feel like a Sardine!
!!

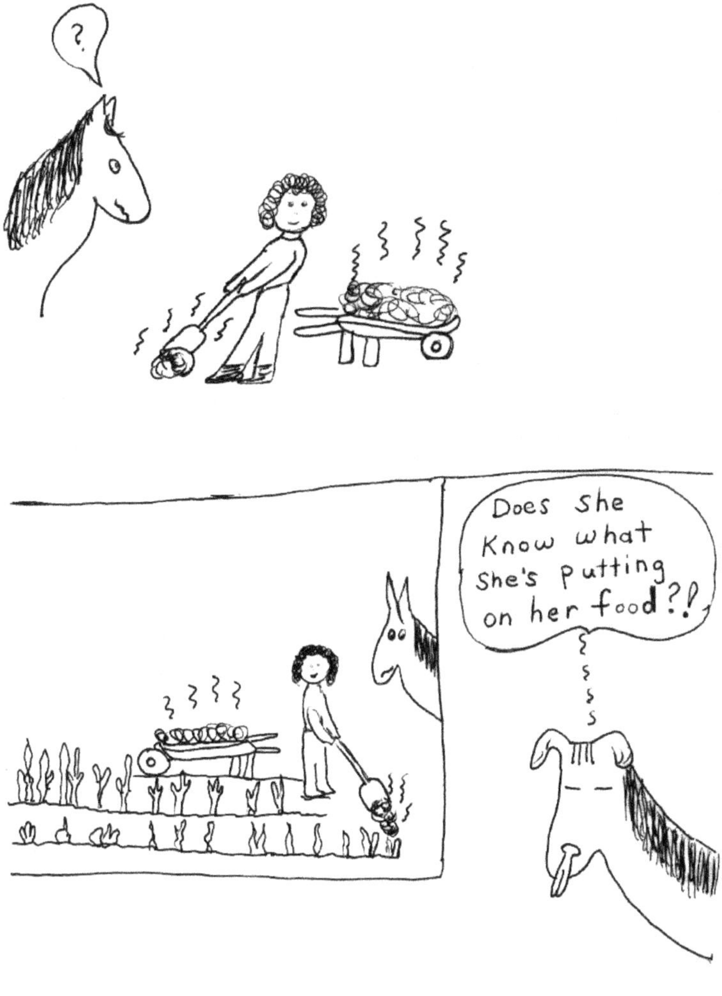
?
Does she Know what she's putting on her food?!

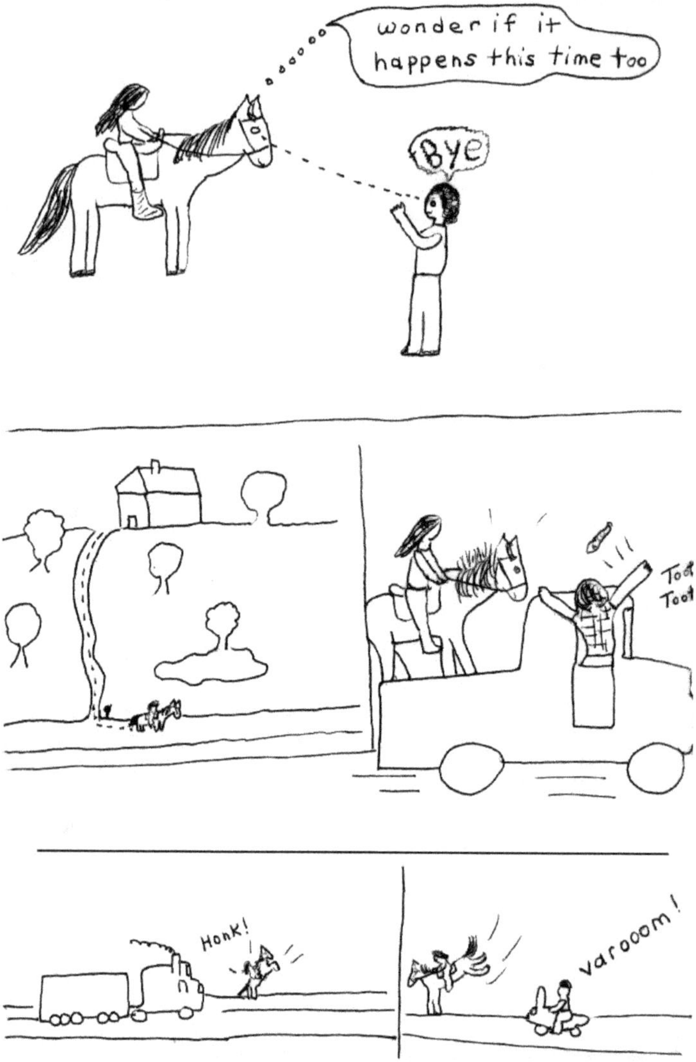
wonder if it happens this time too
Bye
Toot Toot
Honk!
varooom!

yup!
I wonder why her mother looks 10 yrs. older everytime we come back from riding on the highway?

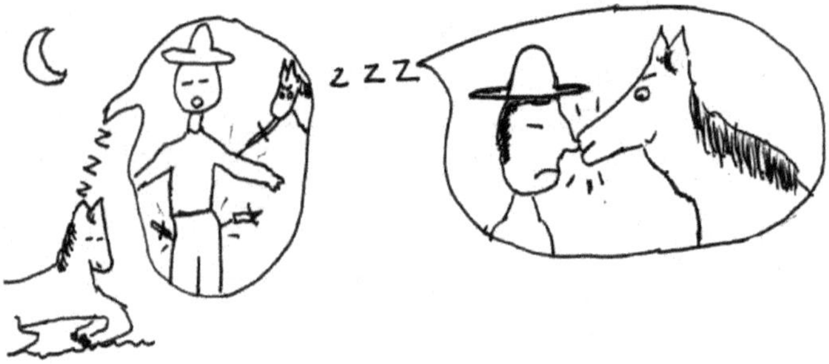
z z Z

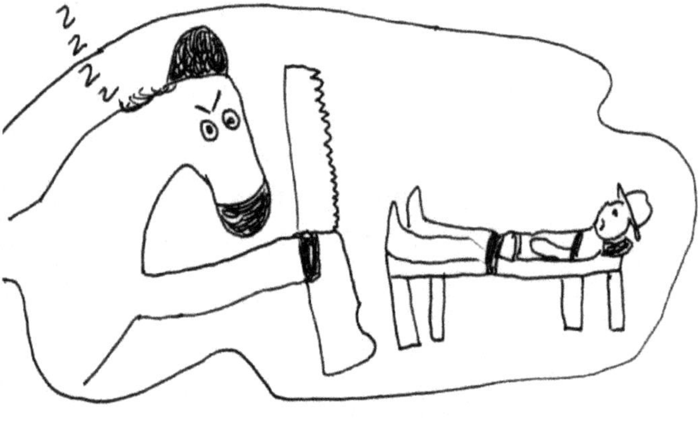

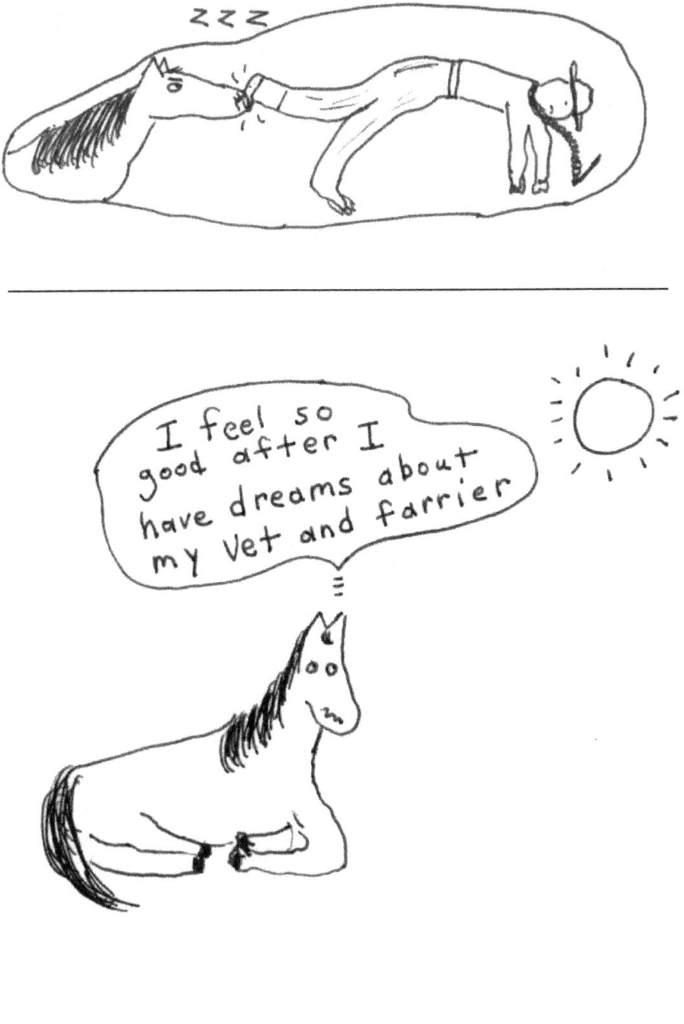
zzz
I feel so good after I have dreams about my vet and farrier

Relax Midnight - it's an exercise wheel!
?
yak yak yak yak
Excuse me!
yak yak yak yak
Hey!!
Isn't this a little too fast!

I think we should put 3 bars on the garden
Come on...
Even 2 bars are High enough to Keep him out.
How low can you go as everybody Limbo Rocks

1

3

2

4

Pucker up...
It's mistletoe
time

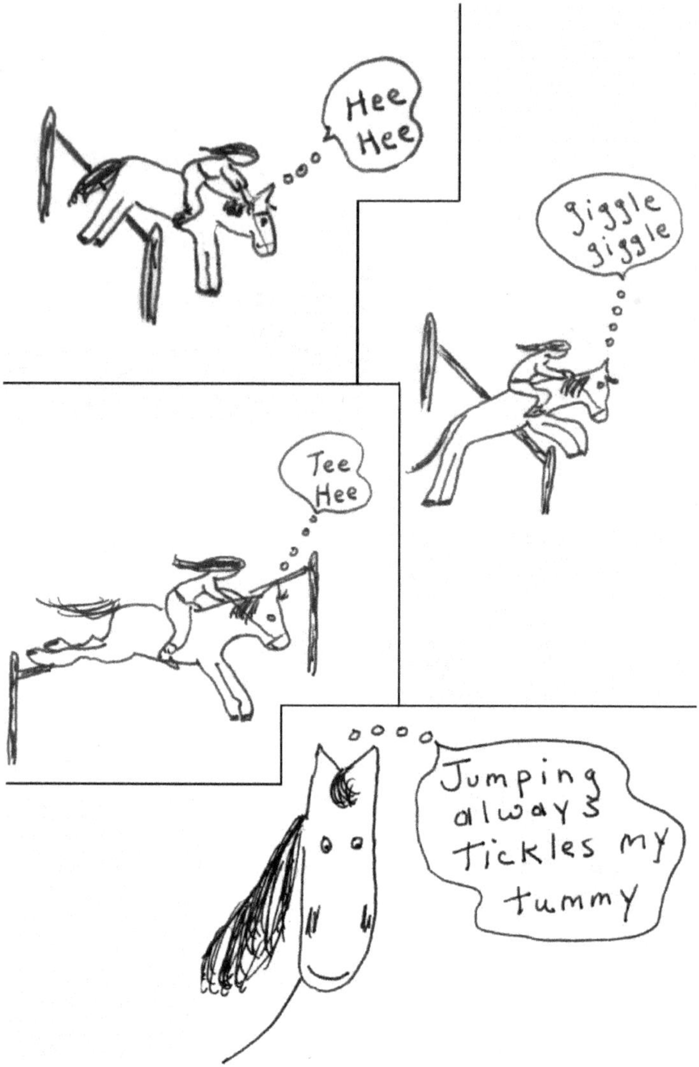
Hee Hee
giggle giggle
Tee Hee
Jumping always tickles my tummy

THANK YOU SIR, FOR LiTTLE girls

www.ingramcontent.com/pod-product-compliance
Lightning Source LLC
Chambersburg PA
CBHW060720030426
42337CB00017B/2938
9780692616550